My Own Wonderland

Ashley Maureena

Copyright © 2018 by Ashley Maureena

All rights reserved. No part of this publication may be reproduced, distributed, or transmitted in any form or by any means, including photocopying, recording, digital scanning, or other methods without the prior written permission of the publisher, except in the case of brief quotations embodied in critical reviews and certain other noncommercial uses permitted by copy law.

Published 2018
Printed in the United States of America
ISBN: 978-1-7328725-0-9
E-ISBN: 978-1-7328725-1-6
Library of Congress Control Number: 2018912140

Cover design by Ashley Maureena

For information, please write:
PhoenixCrossFire Press
PO Box 962
Frisco, TX 75034

www.ashleymaureena.com

*dedicated to my PawPaw,
who always listened to tales of my wonderland*

Contents

Introduction 6
My Own Wonderland 7
The Waiting Groom 8
Badminuteton 8
Wonders of The Dying World 9
Webbed Violin 10
Figurehead 10
Isaac 11
Film Noir 12
Parasite Lost 13
Hot Air Weeds 14
Scrambled Egg 14
Earth Mother 15
The Sun Cries 16
Flakes 18
Puppet Swings 19
Four Horsemen 20
Question Asked 21
Six Months Cold 22
Autumn Field 23
The Light Shines Brightest in the Night 24

Soul's Rest	26
Serengeti	27
Light Bug	28
PSL Rains	30
The Evolution	31
Hammock View	32
Lightning Crashed	33
October	34
Twenty-Three and Divided	35
The River Bank	36
Kilimanjaro Symphony	38
MMXVI	39
Statued Art	41
Lady of Lake	42
The Last of Devoted Love	43
Vitamin C Mirror	44
The Desert's Palm	46
Snow White	48
Quetzalcoatl's Pyramid	49
Maiden's Journey	50
Acknowledgements	56
About the Author	57

Introduction

Whether I was in the piney woods of southeast Texas or the foothills of the, my childhood mind would create a magical land around me. Inspired by Anne Shirley, Laura Ingalls, and Felicity Merriman, I was ready to have adventure. Hiking through the woods on a mountainside led to discovery of small creeks and shallow caves. A natural throne made of stone motivated me to claim the whole region as my kingdom. Tree branches danced together and formed the towering peaks of a cathedral; giant stone slabs fell together to create homes for my woodland subjects. The natural wonders my eyes beheld, and the fantastical world my mind built upon them, have stayed in my memory for decades since.

And still I view the world around me with the same fascination. I understand that I do not see the world as others do. A beach is a place of relaxation and peace to my friends, but to me it is a mermaid's lagoon and a pirate's dock. Rabbits in the backyard are not garden-eating pests, but frantic workers with deadlines and an angry wife at home. The world is one part Neverland and one part Wonderland for me. And I hope to share a glimmer of it with you through these forty poems.

My Own Wonderland

Pawprints trace among the sycamore trees,
The wind whistles lowly in gentle breeze,
Katydids hum a melodious tease.
Wonderland shines down in the river pool,
Concave waterfall lips drip nice and cool,
Upon my rocky throne only I rule.
This mountainside kingdom is my domain,
Come fall shades, winter snow, or spring rain,
Nature bows to me so have I ordained.
A wreath of flowers serves me as a crown,
I laugh free mirth for there is none around,
And there I retreat when I'm feeling down.

The Waiting Groom

Sleep eternal slumber oh blanched tree
Sakura blossoms fall to the bridegroom's dream
A ripple in the starlight of his mind
The memory of his loved haunting bride

Badminuteton

Two and two, dance on court,
Laugh so gay, sudden snort.
Gleeful smirk, sound retort.
Birdie fly, soar your wings,
Leisure time, sport of kings,
Divided field of strings.
Trumpet call, up to lips,
Bell unsung, used for hits,
Hand so tight, turn to grips.
Upward wafts music notes,
All aboard their tiny boats,
Gliding free, tempest floats.

Wonders of The Dying World

Desert sands cannot bury you
Six feet under you are not
God-king believed to be true
Preserved riches to rot.
Slaves made your halls of splendor
For artists later to render.

You loved her to eternity
So marble you cased her in
Minarets grand for all to see
But will your riches forgive a sin?
Thirty-two million to starve to death
And join her last breath.

Overlook the sea you braved
But waves couldn't still your heart
You drank his death, built his grave
A tomb that took history's part.
Mausolus we only know your name
For death was your claim to fame.

Webbed Violin

Soft violin plays majestic in the night,
The glow of its strings burning bright,
Entangled webs the cords stretch on man,
In the darkness only he is left to stand,
To take the fall as the others run,
Waits for fate in the morning sun.

Figurehead

Poseidon's queen,
In the deep serene,
Bound by anchor, too blind to see.
Do your arms still rise?
Can you reveal your eyes?
Entangled webs in the deep blue sea.
Jellyfish glide,
Dolphin's ride,
But you stay firm in the seventh sea.

Isaac

Winged-steed of sapphire hue,
Etheral shimmering scales of blue.
Soaring higher, Apollo's mount,
Tail and mane of highest thread count.
A neigh and deepest breath,
From the belly a fiery death.
The heated sky a rainbow makes,
Arching the golden chariot wakes.
Rises above the cloud of mer,
A song it sings without a word.
Notes so soft they drift away,
Giggling, they dance and play.
The end of world island tree,
Where they end their mirthful spree.
Caught in branches and turned to gold,
To pluck the apple one must be bold.
Or rest below the laden boughs,
In doldrum thought, begins to drowse.
Then suddenly a wind does stir,
Sending apple into a sudden hurl.
Upon the head of the man astute,
Gravity, all in the name of fruit.

Film Noir

The rain beats down on the back alleyway,
Trolley spins its wheels and hills away,
From a lonesome neon sign a flick and pop,
Another letter in a name has dropped.
Cigarette smoke and the stir of ice,
Sounds of jazz makes the darkness bright,
A pair of lovers who fall into embrace,
Drop umbrellas to dance in place.
Her slender neck and cello heels,
Bend back under his sax and steel,
"Your notes are all in tune with mine;
Say we'll be together for all of time."

Parasite Lost

Parasite runs on surface red
Flicking quickly
He hunts the dead.
In muslin his body wrapped
Thick and tight
His heart is trapped.
Bandaged face has no eyes
White cloth blinds
And protects all lies.
Legs and arms jointed bends
Down on fours
More monsters than men.
World around them all burn
Dust and soot
End times all churn.

Hot Air Weeds

Sail away, little mite man,
Go so far, go where you can.
A top hat basket,
And dandelion casket,
As the breeze spreads seeds into the air.
Sing a song, little proud man,
Boast yourself, gather your fans,
Your hot air balloon,
And tune of your bassoon,
As the wind sings strings without a care.

Scrambled Egg

Humpty Dumpty, please run fast,
Your thin shell is as fragile as glass,
Time chases hard with a fist on ground,
A hammer and hand better to pound.
Another egg scrambled to die,
Another chance for life, goodbye.
Year after year, all the world's men,
Never put the princess together again.
The king and his horses foiled the plan,
Destroy the egg before life began.

Earth Mother

Scream aloud, Mother Queen,
Soaring high, your servants be.
Ruling sky, Your Command,
Ne'er soldier out of hand.
Flying loops, ovaled clouds,
Higher up, few and proud.
Frozen springs from your eyes,
Crystal blue, royalty cries.
Canopy green on your head,
Men kill you, cut you dead.
Gasp for breath, do not bleed,
From your mouth endless stream.
Soot and dust churn your burns,
Grind powder into homes.
Towers tall trap inside,
Unfaithful few, run and hide.
Mercy begs, fall from grace,
Ending now human race.
Mother Queen she returns,
Reset all, her heart yearns.
With, without, she carries on,
You are with her or you're gone.
All her time, no game lost,
Always win, any cost.

The Sun Cries

The normal radiant sun,
Its beams once shining bright,
Thinks of the barrel of a gun,
She knows that end is not right.

Tears fall down, salted rain,
Down to lake, once so fresh,
Life sustaining, all her brain,
An ink blot on designer dress.

Fish cannot live in such place,
The salt strong, dead sea rises,
But winter needles make a face,
Life pushes on despite a crisis.

A bat leaps out from the tree,
The last light of sun calls out,
His signal stands for all to see,
But the dark night is all about.

The fighter and his cross-crowned friend,
Circle the stars with laser shots,
Light and dark to make amends,
Balance spoken, but never brought.

No moon shines in deadly scene,
Planet destroyed for power race,
Millions die and millions bleed,
Pieces fall to mourn in daze.

Brothers, friends, swords are drawn,
Fire, lava, the earth it quakes,
The sun she knows it is wrong,
Cries her song to eternal lake.

Flakes

Slowly falling throughout the night
To end long journey's flight.
A shooting star that's made of ice,
Crystal cold, landing, pay the price.
The moment's beauty now turned to tears,
Melted to mere whisper in another's ears.
Truly this sprite did exist?
No, nothing more than winter's kiss.

Puppet Swings

Swinging along little puppet boy,
On the dead man's tree,
The yo-yo red balloon toy,
Playing always, never free.
Above the smog cloud horizon,
Like the prize gold egg,
The dreary sun crawling arises,
Hand, arm, torso, foot, and leg.
Branches curve to touch ground,
Marionette falls low,
His spirits tumble further down,
Dewdrop tears now flow.

Four Horsemen

Cyborg brain, no thought, trapped in a cell,
Silence – yes, no – your secrets to tell.
Machine or human, the logic compute,
Whatever you choose, your voice is mute.
Opposition, transition, change, believe,
Divide, conquer, our unity we cleave.
Web like a spider, together tangled,
Blinders to see from only one angle.
Five seconds to win a lifetime lost,
One forty characters an unsightly cost.
Acid and death for news travels swift,
Wider we grow, fall down through a rift.
Friend for a moment, enemy for life,
White horse has come to cause all our strife.
The rider's bow pierces hot quacking arrows,
Red horse cometh so prepare the old barrows.
Blood on ice we shall cry for the more,
Vengeance is sweet the crowd loves the gore.
Satiated not for the destruction at hand,
Black rider comes to trample the land.
Scales he has to weigh all you hold dear,
Enjoy these moments for your end draws near.
Death rides silently upon a pale horse,
You started this path with your divisive course.

Question Asked

Left hand explosion,
Heart cries in vain,
Mental commotion,
Girl are you sane?
Thunderous clap,
Volcano explode,
Casted soul trap,
Install cheat code.
'What do you think'
Question is asked,
'Gone in a blink;
Our time has passed.'
Could that be so?
Doom before start?
How can he know,
Without my heart?
'Lies!' I do claim,
Words to not say,
Because not same,
With guilt I do pay.
Paladin Rogue,
Opposite twins,
Please launch the drogue,
Landing, he wins.

Six Months Cold

Persephone journeys to Hades
And summer's bliss fades.
Mother Winter shrouds her head,
Protection from all that is dead.
Turin's image to rise again,
Phoenix fire that burns all sin.
Wisping hair like banshee wails
The golden leaves and snowflakes fell.
Daisy petals turn to dust
Countryside is ambered rust.
Sky is torn in shades of gray
Quietly ends November day.

Autumn Field

Fox kit runs along the river bed,
Pebbles and stone, smooth and cool,
Frolicking dance his grinning head.
Grass sways among the leaves,
Squid-like arms bend and reach,
Shifting daftly the parting seas.
Over the flock assembled commands,
Scarecrow in her ragged dress,
Arms crossed, so stoic she stands.
Wrapping about, braided boughs,
Slither upward into the clouds,
Forever faithful, wedding vows.
Among the twigs there is a face,
Sullen, somber, eternal, unchanged,
Yet perfect ivory, jaded grace.

The Light Shines Brightest in the Night

Twinkle, twinkle star shine bright,
The light shines brightest in the night.
Above the stable, above the house,
Painted white, the color now doused.
Rose garden speech for all to hear,
But sadly there is no one near.

Survival they now seek to find,
Survival is all upon their mind,
Survival now for all of time.

In the forest they hunt and play,
To rest from work, their live they pay.
Archer green, his bow held high,
Aims at his foe, snake slides by.
The creature shrieks and hisses too,
But arrow passes coils right through.

Snake he lives another day,
Snake he hates when men pray,
Snake enjoys the death foray.

Through the coil arrow flies,
Into a sheep, it now dies.
Its coat, its skin, bad wolf takes.
Its thought and life bad wolf fakes.
Marches down to little pig's home,
Huffs and puffs for brand new bone.

Little pig watches from his chair,
Little pig can only stop and stare,
Little pig – do you even care?

Outside his slop grows cold,
Hungry pig, but never bold.
Yet the slop is waste from lips
Of Microphone that spits and hiss.
Eat up this talking point waste,
Little pig gladly does fill his face.

The slop grows stale but eat it still,
The slop tastes bland, get your fill,
The slop – enjoy, your last meal.

Soul's Rest

A patch of black nests
Over window, soul's rest,
Obsidian orb reflects light,
Outlined thick of sigh.
Shadows cast over river vale,
Slithers down on to hell:
Barbed silence wire
To cross Lucifer's fire.
River turns to twisted snake.
His two heads, Forked and Raked,
Case the rat into the trap,
For amusement of Top Ol Hat,
Who laughs and grins,
To catch another's sin.
His monocle eye peers
And sees your deepest fears.
His privilege tower highly sets
The flower which casts the net:
A field of stars set for bait.
A young couple, lying, wait,
On blanket's back, far apart,
Unable to stop the beating heart.
Closer two move to dance,
Breath heavy with the chance.
Above patch of black nests,
Closes window, souls rest.

Serengeti

In golden fields the wind swept thru,
Gentle stalks sway with summer's dew,
Every step taken, the crickets flew,
Taste of life fresh in world so new.
Majestic how he walks the plains,
Part before him you mighty grains,
Slow and purpose the pachyderm reigns,
Marching always onward in campaigns.
He trumpets brilliant to the morning sky,
A thousand doves hear his mourning cry,
Spreading wings, take air they fly,
Soaring graceful, they ride so high.
Dip low, dear birds, away from sun,
Learn from Icarus before you're done,
Swoop down to earth, take leg and run,
Plant yourself, don't be outdone.
By the flowers who are smiling bright,
Reds, yellows, blues – oh the sight:
Little petals, no, do not take flight,
Why must we run on, oh eternal plight.

Light Bug

Dear light bug had disappeared
But he's back for 'nother year,
To lead me to the bleak abyss:
The hallowed hall of fog and mist.
My destiny – shall I face
In this cold, demented place?
Alone I stand in the dark,
No sound but my beating heart.
Faint glimmer ahead – is it him?
My guiding light bug, oh so dim.
Before I would always stray,
Blindly, to find my way.
Falling down on broken limbs,
Bleeding wounds on broken skin.
Stubborn, steadfast, stand my ground,
All to see no one there around –
Light bug gone, no guide to shine
To the destiny that was mine.
But is he here to show the way?
Will there be morning to this day?
Dull image, muscle, proud, blood – hart,
Is this the goal or merely a start?
Is this the answer deep in my mind,
To this hart and me his hind?
Eyes open, he notes and darts,
Please, no, still my heart,
Should I pursue or watch him go?
To stay alone or be his doe?
Light bug, light bug or where are thee?
Why have you abandoned me?

I do not know which path to take,
To stay alone, my heart to ache?
Or chase him down, my heart to break?
Open my eyes, please awake!
Falling faster, ever down,
My feet, I'm free, no solid ground.
Further lithe stag he 'scapes,
My heart, his hooves do traipse.
The pain, it hurts, it must end,
Oh, light bug, please, vision send,
Clairvoyance, I need it now,
For answers are naught to found.
Fleeting, further...
        Further...
                Down I spill.
                Further...
                        Crashing, no movement. Still.

PSL Rains

Sweet
        Sweet
Green grass tickles the porous skin
Absorbs the flood as the season begins
The sky opened to the rain
Down it cries again and again

Spice
        Spice
The orange it enters into food untold
Addicted all the spice must flow
Cult follows the two-tailed queen
Pumpkin rapture toward heavenly glow

The Evolution

Radiant sun shining bright,
Blocked by heaven's gazing might.
Eyes piercing down upon the plain,
Powerful beams fall on she who reigns.
A crown turned halo be –
An angel queen is she?
Maiden dressed in splendor,
Or a pawn made to hinder?
How dazed her eyes appear –
Her love cries so softly near;
Tears of life that hit rippled rings.
Freedom – an impossible dream!
He emerges from water's depths,
And ever gently up he crept,
Charles, alas, you may be right!
For this tiny creature is now a sight.
Tooth and claw is bared,
Easily he climbs the air.
Eyes who pierced before
Will suddenly pierce no more,
As heaven's gazing might,
Turns to silent, deadly night.

Hammock View

The platypus grins and sings a sweet tune,
As he dances merrily for month of June.
The dandelion atop his furry head sways,
As a warm wind blows in, late from May.
Plucked one by one, notes on a staff,
Soar up for the sky, like neck of giraffe.
The monkey he hears, in his coconut tree,
The harmony plays on, summer's symphony.
Excited – he howls in delight!
The coconuts tremble, oh what a fright.
Too frightened to stay anymore,
One breaks away and falls to the floor.
Into the ocean it plunges in depth,
Alone in the dark, slowly he wept.
The fish he could take no more wet salt,
And jumped for new life in one giant vault.
His next ocean in delight did smile
And extended a rainbow to beam for awhile,
The rainbow it spread to the clouds up above,
Who released sweet kisses, wrapped up in love.
Oh down little morsels, sweetly they whirl.
All the way down, straight to this girl.

Lightning Crashed

Three flames quiver, shining bright,
Out of darkness, deep in night.
Alley Cat now lifts his head,
A song to sing, honor lost and dead.
Wisdom of his words ring true,
To Vigilant Owl, asking him "Who?"
Perched aloft the sickly tree,
Swaying kindly in the breeze.
Angels how they listen in
To hear of hearts break and mend.
Their jubilance or so it seems,
Transcends down, radiant beams.
The flowers lift leaves so high
And cheerfully they start to sigh.
Voices joined together soar
Higher, stronger winds, a storm.
Cyclone revolves faster still.
Lightning tremble. Sudden chill.
He looks at her, she at him,
Bated breath and pulls her in.
The lightning bursts, reflects,
The glint of his on the left,
Quietly now she sighs.
Nevermore to say goodbye.

October

A mane of six surround the face,
Violet, blue, all gentle grace.
Golden glow, a smile beams,
As she dances in the breeze.
Arms wave to her own tune,
In the spring she fully blooms.
Yet further still, roots descend,
Unseen to all, trapped within:
Forked tongue hiss and sting,
Reptilian friend, angelic wings,
Slithers out of captive cage,
Sliced so clean before its age.
Woodsman's axe fallen swift,
Crimson blood, south it drips.
Three long drops into the fire,
Cloven tongues consume the pyre.
A death which comes this soon,
Leads to more, a birth anew.
With a screech, phoenix rises
To the sky, a tear advises.

Twenty-Three and Divided

Enraptured in roots
With no understanding
Cottonmouth snakes
Do all the explaining.
Poor little sheep
Are herded like cattle
Continental plates
To dine on and prattle.
"This doesn't make sense!"
But did you read the book?
The one teacher gave
For the history you took.
Learn for yourself
Ignore sheep in wolves' clothes
They drive you to cliffs
And fall off in droves.

The River Bank

Man walks on legs of four,
Always moving forevermore,
Extra legs, beams of steel,
Staying in place, the rolling wheel,
Chasing the cake from rod and reel.

Lazy devil sets his bait in stone,
Lays back upon his beach chair throne.

The sun lures him to sleep,
His Z's he no longer keeps,
They run away into the air,
But lazy devil, he doesn't care,
That they'll be trapped, ensnared.

Like butterflies caught in a net,
They shake, afraid, and start to fret.

Children laugh, dance, and play,
Enjoying their new "catch of the day",
Merrily they dance around,
Imps now hold Lucifer's Crown,
In their mirth, they will drown.

Tears of joy stream from their eyes,
Roll down hill where the river lies.

Upon the hazy shore,
Man walks on legs of four,
Limbs that burst into fragile wings,
As the coming dusk learns to sing,
The bullfrog thumps his long bass string.

The oak tree shadow begins to form,
A lurid slug, but salt I pour.

Kilimanjaro Symphony

Treble clef smoke off mountain top
A melody rises in the breeze
A rest, legato quarter raindrop
Stand back! Elephant is going to sneeze!
Across Serengeti the tuba rumbles
Staccato antelope sprint away
Bee joins the song with a bumble
Watch out! Stampede choir serenade the day!
Gilded horns glisten on buck
Eight notes counted on notched string
Do, re, mi – the harp we pluck
Quiet now! The silent stag will sing!
Trumpet vines rise forty-five degrees
Trampled before, won't stay down
High C call, listen to pleas
'We are! Brazen, the greatest of sound!'
Timpani frogs and bass drum toads
Cranes sing soprano, arrogant bird
Nature's wild symphony off of the road
Sweet song! Most glorious any has heard.

MMXVI

Through Bluegrass, wind does blow,
Mockingbird sings of woe,
Darkened skies open to Purple Rain,
Vanity,
She feels no pain.
Careless Whisper is in the breeze,
Dancing Butterfly, Stinging Bee,
Hazy summer comes to an end,
And The Priest,
He found his friend.
A glistened throne holds the Queen,
And the Princess looks in between,
She got caught up in the flood,
But Yellowcoat,
Covers her own blood.
Albatross and Eagle watch from above,
After the years they found their dove,
The peace she brings is final hope,
Suffered long,
This time we cope.

Candyman greets the Little One,
'Come with me and we'll have some fun!',
Mom and Dad they join in,
Imagination,
Where have you been?
Wonder Woman flies to the sky,
And Professor wonders why,
No spell on earth can cure his pain,
Then Stardust,
Transcends another plane.
And all the Federales say,
Pancho now has gone away,
All the outlaws are heading home,
And Lefty,
He's all alone.
Starglider he's the last to go,
He's flying higher with the crow,
Guiding all those we love still,
We miss them,
We always will.

Statued Art

Statue silent, granite heart,
Treated cold, simple art,
Hands upon her eyes
No tears but still she cries.
None see her quiet pain
Aches she feels in marble vein.
He bought her in pretense,
A kind word, romantic gist.
For once, love, she believed,
But now knows, she's deceived.
A statue, silent, all for view
Boast piece, an ego coup.
Unheeded her stone heart,
Merely another piece of art.

Lady of Lake

Deceitful face, forward and back,
Sand-covered feet, heartless and black.
Velveteen antlers, shed gilded disguise,
Lady of Lake, fell for his lies.
Cheetal look down, your spots are a ring,
Bound to those claims, you never will sing.
Maiden of Water, she bears it so dear,
He sprints away, she'll never come near.
Panthers and tigers, they wish to play,
Chief doesn't mind, he'll give her away.
Jealous the titans, stroke beards in thought,
All maidens to them, their beauty they bought.
Silver-tongued words, to a lonely heart blue,
Gentle whispers, so carefully cooed.
Maiden take sword, rise from your fate,
Protect yourself, no champion awaits.
Flowers do fade, every rose has a thorn,
Armor yourself, false affections do scorn.
Huntress she is, now seated on perch,
Eyes always search, for the cheetal, her first.

The Last of Devoted Love

None can find such devoted love,
Like the Phoenix and the Turtledove.
When in one's death, the other flames,
How to live on when heart is slain?
The Bard wrote of this tragic tale,
When all birds mourned in full regale:
Oh, woe to world, and woe to love,
That we lost Phoenix and Turtledove.
Together they who stood so grand,
Proudly walked in perfection's hand.
Ne'er did hearts prove thus true,
As when this love bloomed and grew.
To stranger no eye would stray,
For devoted were their hearts to stay.
Entwined in life, so entwined in death,
Embraced their wings for final breath.

Vitamin C Mirror

Atlas shrugged the world away
And turned the darkness into day.
Intercepted star, the solaris disc,
To bring all light, dangerous risk.
Photo beams float to the sky,
A mane of gold for the diamond pie.
Warming arms, scented like yellow,
Softens celestial puffs of marshmallow.
Juiced like an orange, out it pours,
Vitamin C in a mirror it stores.
The mirrored reflection, always a change,
Rippled and tides to a world rather strange.
Sphinx looks on – disdainful, amused,
Feu de canon! His nose is now bruised!
Metals and stones can never replace,
The solemn defiance of lion's face.

Agitated, his tail lifts on high,
Ringing the dinner bell attached to the sky.
Clanging about the tether pole's neck,
That rod leading up from Steps of Aztec.
Nimble Jack flies through all of the stairs,
To play tether bell with nary a care.
His heart out of pocket does fall,
To the maiden Jill who beckons his call.
Tumbling ever after her fairy tale lad,
Never an ending, torn hearts always sad.
Crows circle two flying higher and higher,
Giving souls they carry to richest buyer.

The Desert's Palm

Blazing gold above the sky
Melodic wind heard on high
Sweeping o'er the desert dunes
Softly now brings a tune
To the palm whose dance on air
Forbidden temptress, naught to care
The desert sands about her race
Reaching up her skin of grace
Circling her body; she moves
The lust of desert all consumed
Eyes of fire piercing gaze
Leaves him breathless in a haze
Confusion on the desert's part
But the palm continues her own art

Like twist of hip, raise of hand
Desert swells, with kiss of sand
Wind displaces her leaves of hair
Desert inhales, can't help but stare
Every sway a lure in trance
Faster now her tempting dance
Desert now can hardly breathe
With this wicked company
Sand traces along her skin
Captures her, a vengeful grin
Her chest billows below his hand
Lost she is, to desert sand

Snow White

A candle burning in the night,
Among darkness seems so bright.
Reveals wrongs that feel so right:
Confliction. Morals. Eternal fight.
Panther eyes can pierce the soul,
Stir emotions, consume you whole.
Caramel's sweet but tastes of salt,
On such skin you find no fault,
Serpent twists around Snow White
Enter in, so small, so tight.
Seven dwarves live here no more,
An apple falls upon the floor.
With a gasp her body aches
Poison spreads, begins to shake.
Moaning as she feels consumed,
Spinning now is the room.
Collapsed she lays so still
With your hands did you kill?
Below her lays the soaking pool
A drink so time, it makes you full.
Satisfied lips speak softer now
Charming's kiss, awoken vow.
Opened orbs take pleasure in
Panther eyes and caramel skin,
Ever after for Snow White,
All the wrongs that feel so right.
Among darkness shines so bright,
A candle burning in the night.

Quetzalcoatl's Pyramid

The golden sun hangs low on you so grand
Granite blocks climbing high to the sky
What god did you serve to demand
The march of children and their mother's cry?

A beating heart in hand sacrifice
The crimson flow from the obsidian throne
Jaguar's honor has paid the price
For the living dead whose pain loudly moans.

Feathered serpent your forked-tongue flies
Your priest take the beautiful best for slaves
How many in your name did die
To be buried in their lakeside graves?

Maiden's Journey

Azure field, majestic in the sky,
Beseeches heart to take wing and fly.
Only hope sits upon coral throne,
Two-headed king far away from home.
Her journey shall take her many days,
For he lives a thousand miles away.
The first step is the hardest one,
Blindly goes into the rising sun.

Cattle and gently rolling hills,
Give way to trees and wisp-o-wills.
Dark forest fears of the great unknown,
Brings the doubt of leaving home.
But her love of king is strong,
She gains her courage and continues on.
Bayou swamps and enormous toads
Begin to greet her on the road.

No passage to her they give,
For fair maiden with them will live.
Disgusted by such a lurid fate,
Pelican saves with the meal he ate.
The guttural beak now full and fat,
Waves her forward to Golden Cat.
Violet stripes upon golden body,
Tiger stands noble – fierce and haughty.

"Little Mouse, why do you stand,
Here in the court of my Bayou Land?
Surely from the west you hail,
Land of horns, yes, we know it well."

And with a nod of his striped face,
Two scaly guards did take their place.

"Your land is dear and helped our need,
Now my turn to repay their deed.
Please accept these reptilian steeds,
And through my land you shall speed."

Graciously, maiden accepted aid,
And the alligators swiftly sped away,
Through the sole of Bayou Land
'Til Magnolia did take a stand.

"Dear Bird, you may pass through me,
But your hungry friends are to leave.
For the boar who call me home,
Would rather wish to be left alone.
And the fish who swim and play,
Prefer, like cats, to sleep all day."

Maiden bid her friends good-bye,
And entered in where rebels lie.
Quietly, she did proceed,
To not disturb the silence of the trees.
Hours and hours, the woods grew dense,
The air weighed and her fear intensed.
In the distance – a wonderous call!
The ground shook and the trees did fall.

Charging through, an elephant herd,
Lead by a bear against a mighty bird.
Blood and iron did fill the air,
Curiously, she stopped to stare.
The eagle spread its imposing wings,
A cry for war against pachyderm fiends.
Many rallied on either side,
Maiden left before the tide.

The thunderous trumpet of cavalry charge,
Sounded through the land at large.
Battlefield was left behind,
For the coast and the Dolphin Isle.
The dolphins there did all agree,
The quickest route would be by sea.
Upon their backs she did seat,
Crystal waves lapped 'round her feet.

A song of hope left the maiden's mouth,
And in their glee, the dolphins shout.
For to their arena of their world,
Were they taking this lone girl.
Turquoise and orange would she see,
And perhaps one day she'd be their queen!
But the hurricanes they had another plan,
For no outsider was wanted in their land.

The wind it howled and precipitously blew,
Maiden unsaddled and off she flew.
Entered in to the magic place,
Talking mice did give her chase.
Down the castle steps she sped,
Where she discovered the frozen head.
With the threat of flame and heat,
The mice conceded their defeat.

Safe passage to her king's domain,
Granted despite all the wind and rain.
Her journey's end is growing near,
All her love for the king to hear.
Truth and devotion did she present,
But in his heart there grew resent,
For another long before,
Had his love all to scorn.

So the double-headed king decrees,
He'll stay in his castle by the sea,
For love of a maiden means nothing,
While he wears the poisoned ring,
Of the dark one he once revered,
To fall for another he now fears.
Has the maiden come thus far,
For her heart to be disarmed?

Acknowledgements

I want to thank all my family, friends, and educators who have believed in me and prepared me along my journey. An exceptional thanks to my parents who have been my emotional, mental, spiritual, and financial supporters. A thank you to my PawPaw and Grandma, who, while no longer with us, worked with me at a young age to get me where I am today. My beta-readers Joci, Buck, and Charliebug – thank you for your friendship and patience with my repetitive questions. Finally, to Alyssa, Britt, and my church family for their encouragement and prayers, thank you. God has used so many of you to keep me moving forward.

To all: I love you.

About the Author

Ashley Maureena is a resident of the 'best US city to live in' Frisco, Texas, where she enjoys the excitement of city life, Friday night lights, and sprawling ranch land all within twenty minutes of home. When not processing paper in a cubicle, she explores her native Texas and caters to her cat's every wish. Ashley holds a degree in History and Education from the University of Texas at Dallas and served in the public-school system and non-profit sector. Please feel free to follow her on social media or drop a line.

www.ingramcontent.com/pod-product-compliance
Lightning Source LLC
Chambersburg PA
CBHW031503040426
42444CB00007B/1197